The Mis... Mystery

by Cheryl Ryan • illustrated by Holly Cooper

HARCOURT BRACE & COMPANY

Orlando   Atlanta   Austin   Boston   San Francisco   Chicago   Dallas   New York
Toronto   London

Bowser wasn't in his cage.

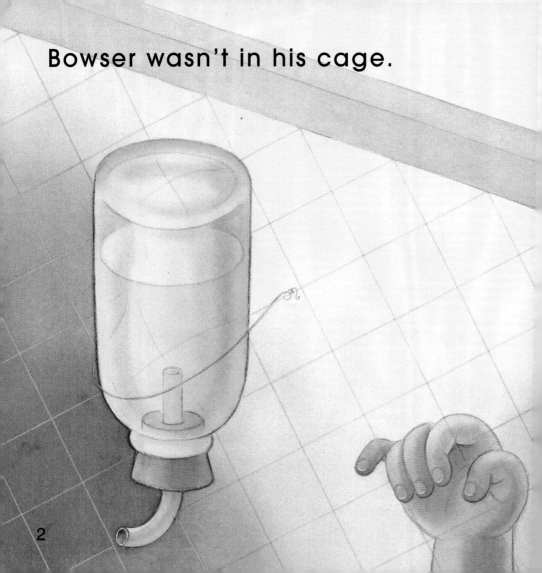

Gina looked all around the cage—
on the right and on the left.

"Bowser is not in his cage," whispered Gina. "What will he do without food?"

4

Reggie looked all around the kitchen. "Where would Bowser go?" he wondered.

"Bowser is not in his cage!"
said Reggie. "What will he do
without water?"

Kyle looked all around the laundry room. "Where would Bowser go?" he wondered.

"Bowser is not in his cage!"
said Kyle. "What will he do without
you?"

Honey looked [in the] garage. "Where [...] thought Honey.

"Where would b[e] Mom."

9

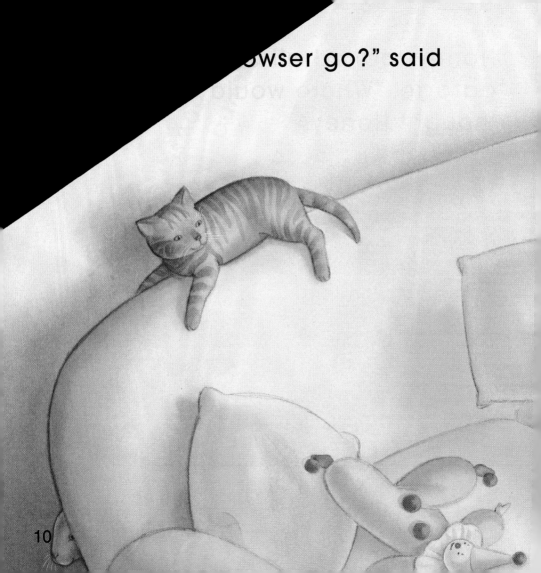

owser go?" said

She looked all around the family room.

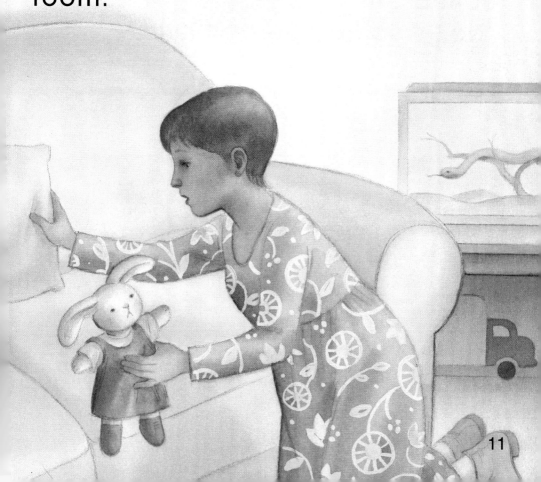

"Has anyone found Bowser?"
called Gina.
"No," said Reggie and Kyle.

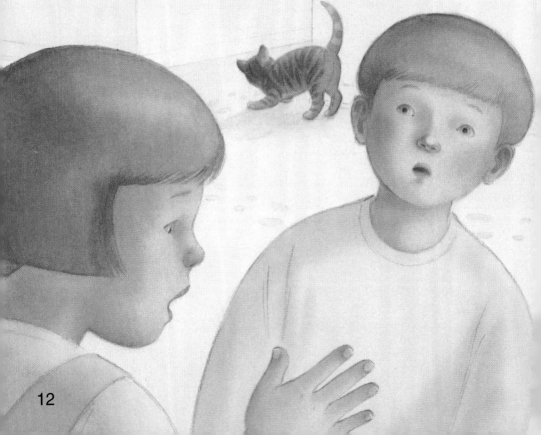

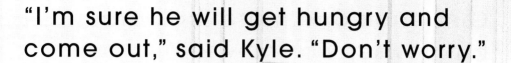

"I'm sure he will get hungry and come out," said Kyle. "Don't worry."

13

Gina took one more look around—
but Bowser was nowhere to be
found.

"What will I do without Bowser? What will he do without me?" she wondered.

She sat down on her bed and let out a loud "Howdy Bowser!"